Eternal Love

Eternal Love

Poems from the First 70 Years

by Lolita L. Jardeleza

Foreword by Robert L. McCreary OFM Cap.

RESOURCE *Publications* · Eugene, Oregon

ETERNAL LOVE
Poems from the First 70 Years

Resource Publications
An Imprint of Wipf and Stock Publishers
199 W. 8th Ave., Suite 3
Eugene, OR 97401

www.wipfandstock.com

PAPERBACK ISBN: 978-1-7252-5758-0
HARDCOVER ISBN: 978-1-7252-5759-7
EBOOK ISBN: 978-1-7252-5760-3

Manufactured in the U.S.A.   JANUARY 8, 2020

To all the fruits of our shining, astonishing, and beautiful love,
with a paean of praise and gratitude to the Lord

God's gifts put man's best dreams to shame.

—Elizabeth Barrett Browning
  Sonnets from the Portuguese #26

Contents

Foreword by Robert L. McCreary OFM Cap. | xi

Acknowledgments | xiii

PART I—LOVE GROWS | 1

1950—ONCE UPON A TIME . . . | 3

1951—REASONS | 4

1952—LITTLE ONE | 5

1953—ANTICIPATION | 6

1954—HISTORY | 8

1955—HOW WISE YOU ARE | 9

1956—WE MANAGE | 10

1957—OBSERVATION | 11

1958—INSURANCE | 12

1959—AS OTHERS SEE US | 13

1960—WE ARE EVEN | 14

1961—PORTIUNCULA | 15

1962—I'M A CLOCKWATCHER | 16

1963—HOW DO YOU DO THAT? | 17

1964—IT'S FOR REAL | 18

1965—I'VE GOT TO CROW! | 19

1966—FRIEND | 21

1967—THANK YOU, DARLING | 23

1968—PRIMARY FUNCTION | 24

1969—HAPPY EIGHTEENTH | 25

1970—THAT'S WHY I REMIND THEM | 26

1971—LOVESONG TO GOD | 27

1972—BALANCE | 28

PART II—LIFE FLOWS | 29

1973—HAPPY TWENTY-SECOND | 31

1974—DELIBERATION | 32

1975—INVITATION | 33

1976—WHAT DO THEY CALL THIS AIR MANEUVER? | 34

1977—LINES ON SURFING | 35

1978—LOGIC | 36

1979—PREFERENCE | 37

1980—HE SET THE PRECEDENT | 39

1981—YOUR GIFT | 40

1982—INVENTORY | 41

1983—VALENTINE | 42

1984—THIS IS WHY | 43

1985—MY TALENT | 44

1986—OH, WOW! | 45

1987—THE SHADOWS FALL | 46

1988—REFLECTIONS ON COMMITMENT | 47

1989—WHAT IS LOVE? | 48

1990—PROBLEMS IN MEASUREMENT | 49

1991—DIAGNOSIS | 50

1992—THANK YOU STILL AGAIN | 51

1993—NEW REASON | 52

1994—THE SHADOWS RETURN | 53

1995—I AM A REALIST | 54

PART III: ON TO ETERNITY | 55

1996—WHAT IS SPOUSAL LOVE? | 57

1997—NOT YET | 58

1998—MOONSCAPE | 60

1999—LAMENT | 61

2000—HAPPY FORTY-NINTH! | 62

2001—MADANG SONG | 63

2002—I WONDER | 64

2003—INDIVISIBLE | 65

2004—BITTERSWEET | 66

2005—DECISION | 67

2006—RETREAT REFLECTION | 68

2007—INESCAPABLE | 70

2008—TEN YEARS AGO, YOU LEFT | 71

2009—RE-DEFINITION | 72

2010—LOVE IS | 73

2011—IMMORTAL BELOVED | 74

2012—LONG DISTANCE LOVE | 75

2013—WILL I EVER GET OVER YOU? | 76

2014—WHO AM I? | 77

2015—HOW? | 78

2016—I AM EQUAL STILL | 79

2017—LAST WALTZ | 80

2018—WIFESONG | 81

2019—PRAYER | 82

Foreword

POEMS ARE ARRANGEMENTS OF words that capture the meaning of a person, of an event, of an experience. A poem can also express meanings hidden in moments of a life. And, when a poem captures these moments in a longstanding relationship like marriage, we find wondrous insight into a life shared. Such are these poems of Lolita Jardeleza, who was married to her Jack for 46 years.

As Lolita's spiritual director since 1971, I am familiar with the raw material that she and the Lord transmuted into verse. What a blessing that now others can share these bursts of wonder into the life force Jack and Lolita shared, as they brought eleven children into the world, into their shared love, and into their love for the Lord!

Lolita's poems are not just sweet memories, though there are such memories. They are also revelations of a sometimes painful, confusing, and hopeful and beautiful love. There are even the wonderful moments when we see how her creative life, as teacher, missionary, mother, and grandmother, manifests her undying love for Jack after he has died.

Each of these poems presents a moment in a long married life. Lolita describes her marriage and her married life as a "Lambent flame that went on to warm both hearth and heart, robust, rowdy, rambunctious." She says "We have enjoyed each other with groaning sideboards, laughter, story-telling and song."

Every poem has a hidden meaning, because the poem reaches more deeply into its moment for a wonder to be shared. Take the time she asked which animal she was like for him (perhaps kitten, or little partridge?) and he replied "a porpoise." That was hardly what she expected! Then he explained more fully: "It is playful, warm and bright." Ever the honest beloved of Jack, she returned that love fully in many ways. She told him, "I love you for all the little ones you planted beneath my heart, living proofs of the love affair between God and you and me."

These memory-poems are beautiful, realistic, and hopeful, and they manifest the graces of a deeply Christian love affair and marriage.

—Father Robert L. McCreary OFM Cap.

Acknowledgments

WITH LOVING THANKS TO my dear friend, great editor, and co-Franciscan Mary Liepold; my childhood buddy and beloved cousin Nonoy Jack Ledesma, who captured our joy in his sketch; to Fr. Robert McCreary for his loving Foreword; and to Yahia Lababidi, who told me the world needs this book of love poems.

PART I—LOVE GROWS

As children of friends, Jack and I met when I was born and he was seven years old. After World War II, he left the Philippines for the U.S. when his mother, who was a POW, was repatriated. We re-met as adults in Washington, D.C., and it was spontaneous combustion on both sides. We courted by correspondence for a year. Then, despite my family's disapproval (I was only 19), we leaped into our life together without looking back, counting only on God's loving grace to see us through. We married in 1951 and had eleven children in fifteen years, six girls and five boys.

We wanted a dozen. Jack was an only child who did not like being an only child, while my mother and my stepmother both grew up with seventeen siblings. The equation in our heads was the same: Big families = lots of fun. God honored our dream by sending our colorful and delightful tribe. We wondered why He hadn't completed the dozen until we realized we always had at least one more around over the years. He saw to that. Praise Him!

"Love comes to some unlooked for, quietly," a poet once said. Ours was dropped into our laps by God when we weren't looking. That lambent flame went on to warm both hearth and hearts of a robust, rowdy, rambunctious family that burgeons merrily down the years. We have thrived on God's unstinting Providence and our enjoyment of each other, with groaning sideboards, much laughter, story-telling and song! Our son Joe says that until he was seven, he thought he was in a musical!

1950—ONCE UPON A TIME . . .

There we were, half a world apart,
Minding our own tidy business, oblivious of each other.
We last saw each other seven years before,
when he was sixteen and I was nine, neither interested in the other.

But God, having one of His very bright ideas, plucked me
from my home and set us in each other's paths
with a casual invitation for a night's tour of the city
that one fine day in June of 1950.

Three hours' pleasant conversation gave us glimpses
of each other's spirits that irrevocably smote us both for life.
Those three hours were followed by a whole year's flurry
of correspondence across the Pacific and found him flying

To my side and launching his blitzkrieg courtship taking me away
with him to be his wife; me burning all my bridges to follow him
across the world in the biggest gamble of my life and stay
with him in a future all unknown, counting only on God to lead the way.

1951—REASONS

I love you
   for your gentle ways,
   for all the many happy days
   you simply give me.

I love you
   for your love of God
   and just like rain on parched sod
   I love your sense of humor.

I love
   your friendly way with every one,
   your easy, childlike sense of fun
   your heart as simple as a star.

I love you
   for your goodness, deep and whole,
   and your tranquility of soul,
   your will to work and fight and win.

I love you
   for your strength of heart—
   but all these reasons are apart
   from my true loving.

I love you most
   because you're mine,
   because you make my whole world shine
   by simply being you, my Darling.

1952 — LITTLE ONE

They tell us now you are coming at last, after all this while.
All at once, it is springtime and living, one sweet smile.
Perhaps 'twas well that you tarried before you came along.
Now we have more to give you, for life is more of a song.

Because he is your Daddy, you will be strong and steadfast and firm,
And for that same, sweet, wonderful reason,
you will be funny, loving, and warm.
Daddy has order to give you—his toy chest is like his mind
With every thing in its right place. Oh, every thing of every kind!

There will be golf balls and bright stones, a fishing pole, a knife
And there will be fun songs and whistles—
the enchantment and magic of life.
Mommy's bundle is different—more like the pocket of all little boys:
Where you'll find a frog and a sunbeam, all sorts of fairyland toys.

You might find a little, lame robin, a star, a little girl's heart,
A tumbleweed rolling along down a meadow, a book, a caramel tart.
So come soon and welcome, our Darling,
Daddy and Mommy are impatient for you!
We have laughter, singing and dancing
to give you your whole life through!

1953—ANTICIPATION

There's a surging singing deep inside me again,
A bursting, a winging from inside me again
A song in my soul,
A vibrance in all
That I hear, that I feel, that I see!

There's a new song escaping my silence today
A teasing, dear melody so easy to play
That says to my heart,
My high, happy heart—
You are coming, soon coming to me!

I have held you within me through moments most dear
Nestled there 'neath my heart, so tiny and near,
But my arms yearn for you,
The softness of you.
Oh hurry, don't tarry, please hurry to me!

Yes, I wait in impatience and breathless, I see
All the brightness and gladness and joy that you'll be,
And I know, yes, I know
God will soon look below
And the floodgates of heaven will be swinging apart

And a miracle sleeping will awaken inside
The blossoming forth of mother from bride,

A child from a love

Created above.

WELCOME, MY DARLING, TO LIFE!

1954—HISTORY

Our marriage first began
In God's mind. There
Like jigsaw puzzles pieces, He
Made all the parts that make up you
And all the parts that make up me.
So when we came across each other
We could see
That all our pieces put together make
Our God's own special jigsaw puzzle—

We.

1955—HOW WISE YOU ARE

"I love you," you had said.
And I, in woman fashion,
Wanting to hear you count the ways
Asked, "Why do you love me? "
"Foolish girl," you said,
"There is no why to loving."

You are so right.

1956—WE MANAGE

We speak two languages, you and I.
We do not always understand what the other
Wants to say.
The "I love you" I say in my verses
You hear in the pies I bake.
You say it in your day-in, day-out patience,
I hear it in the naps you make me take.
I should bake you more goodies—
It would gladden you more
Than words—
But we are what we are.

What does it matter what language we speak,
Or which we better understand?
Over the years we have managed
To get the message across to each other—
Clearly,
Distinctly,
Unmistakably through:
I love you, I love you,
I
Love
You!

1957—OBSERVATION

A nice, warm, pleasant feeling
Love could no more be
Than a rain puddle
can be the sea.

1958—INSURANCE

"I did not marry her for her looks," You said
Of me once.
I was so glad to know that.
So happy to know I need not fear

> The loss of bloom
> Nor wear of time
> Nor the toll that weariness takes

No need to fear
Because I know

My beauty comes from within your heart.

1959—AS OTHERS SEE US

Solomon likened his Beloved to a dove.

Other call their sweethearts "Kitten."

Or "My little partridge."

"If I were an animal which one would I be?"

I asked you and you said,

"A porpoise."

"A porpoise?"—I had not expected that.

"Why, yes!" you said,

"It is playful, warm, and bright!"

1960 — WE ARE EVEN

Do you recall
The year you asked for my help twice?
(It was nearing Christmas.)
The first to buy a present for your mistress,
The next to buy another for your wife.
You winked and said you were so clever
To find both wife and mistress
In the woman of your life.

So?
I am quite clever too.
My paramour and my husband both
Are you.

1961—PORTIUNCULA

With our seventh baby on his way, we knew we had to find more room, and found we had a problem hard to solve—the size of the house we needed did not match what we could afford. We had enough for a house too small for us all. The house that would contain us we could not buy.

But God, as usual, went about doing His thing: a friend knew of a house being sold downtown by its owners and took me there. "This is the one," I thought as I walked in—large, sunny and old-fashioned with a backyard apple tree. We asked good St. Francis to help us and left for our annual vacation to discover upon returning the price had come down to match our money.

We moved in six weeks later and have been here ever since—fifty-eight years, all told, of grace. We named it Portiuncula after Francis of Assisi's first place. Four more babies came through the years. Thirteen of us have enjoyed living here, this warm and welcoming, happy, roomy, laughter-filled space. We like and are grateful for God's ongoing bright ideas—that phenomenon we call grace!

1962—I'M A CLOCKWATCHER

When the fuel gauge reads empty, it's time to fill the tank.
It's time to call the druggist when I am down to one pill.
And when the seconds closer come to twelve and five
I know it's time for love's refill.
Because for eleven years, day in, day out
I could depend, sure as I am alive
That you would telephone me at twelve
And then again, at five.

1963—HOW DO YOU DO THAT?

When we first loved, the way I felt
About you was closer to hero-worship
Than to man-and-woman love.
The years have leveled distances between.
Intimacy, understanding,
The almost total way we know each other
Have banished illusions, and this
Is what I can never thank you for enough—
That through our ups and downs,
You've kept my faith intact
And are my hero still.

1964—IT'S FOR REAL

When you are cross with me and shut me out,
Or angrily storm out of the house,
When you cannot hold the reins in any longer
And let your bitterness wash over me,
     My heart turns cold, hard, bleak and stark.
     I vow I will not let you hurt me anymore;
        To steel myself—be invulnerable,
       And hold my heart away from you.
How resolute I am then!
Until you realize my pain—and you reach out
To draw me in, seeking to heal and soothe the wounds
With gentleness to match. Few words, if any.
Often all you need to do is just
     To hold me close enough to light my heart—

And then its every nook and cranny is shimmering again with joy!

1965—I'VE GOT TO CROW!

I like us.

We go together, you and I.

We fit and match and complement.

If I'm the nut, you're the bolt.

I am steel hard, you are gold.

You are matter of fact. I provide the whimsy.

You are realistic where I would just dream, see?

Your dependability I have colored with surprises;

My fantasies are pungent with your spices.

What a partnership we have!

Because I am impetuous, you've had to be wise.

I am flighty, you are solid. Yours the earth, mine the skies.

I am wishy-washy, you are strong. Yours the substance, mine the song.

I'm the lamp, you my light. Yours, the courage, mine the fight.

With the children, mine the firmness, yours the gentle touch.

With each other, yours the discipline; I goof off too much.

Yours the prudence, mine the faith.

You ensure the graces while I pray.

Yours the caution, mine the hope—you the safeguard of this dope.

Life's dark forces haven't got a chance.

Mine the devotion, yours the romance.

Yours the framework, mine the frills.

We have our cake and eat it too—security with thrills.

I am emotional, you are stable—I just love you as intensely as I'm able.

My ups and downs are leveled by your even, patient ways.

You shine away my tempests with your placid, sunny days.

19

Yet your eruptions are volcanic, mine simply geyser-like,

Enough of light and dark to offset the other's dark and light.

When we work you plod while I look for the kicks in the jobs we have to do.

And the things you enjoy are the things I like because they are fun for you.

My dumb shenanigans do not impress you so I try to give you my best,

As well as love, encourage, and accept you in a life where you can rest.

I look at us and I still cannot get over

How wonderful we are!

Our battles may be lulus but mostly

Our love is like a star—a quiet, shining certitude

That is pure joy.

And in its high, proud, finer moments, why,

Our love is absolutely magic—you and I!

1966—FRIEND

I mainly thought of you as husband,
sweetheart, lover, beau.
I also thought of you as guide,
Scoutmaster, leader, the one
who took me where I had to go,
novice-master, fellow pilgrim,
we did ministry side by side.
Co-parent, roommate, playmate,
emotional crutch,
adversary sometimes, challenger, prod,
always, supreme gift from God.

Wind beneath my wings,
inspiration, desperation,
cause of my singing, my joy!
Teddy bear, grizzly bear,
my old Papa, little boy,
patient, nurse, favorite gourmand,
reformer, nag. Petter, pet,
favorite dancing partner,
guardian human,
listener always there,
sounding board, Safety net.

Like an unbroken thread
in our relationship was the fact
that we were always friends.
I told you everything—I felt I could,

you were so good.
In your faithfulness and tenacity
you never deviated from your loving me
even when, often, I made no sense to you.

A friend, it is said, is one with whom
you can dare to be yourself.
You not only gave me that,
you were the soil where I could grow, bloom, bear fruit.
I thank you for everything you always were for me,
still are, will be without end.
I thank God for the incredible gift of you,
my most beloved, very bestest Friend!

1967—THANK YOU, DARLING

Funny things feed a woman's soul—
> Dandelions clutched by a baby fist…
> A set of oils for Mother›s Day . . .
> An outrageously expensive fancy nightgown
> for our tenth child's birth . . .
Then there was that night
You turned your back to me in bed,
I rubbed your back and then you said,
> "Heaven must be made of you."

I've fed my soul on that for years.

1968—PRIMARY FUNCTION

There was a time when I thought being a good mother meant:
   Instilling my hard-won values in my children's hearts,
   Nourishing their young bodies with good, healthy meals,
   Making sure their clothes and rooms and hearts and minds were clean,
   Providing all those day-in, day-out things mothers do—
   Affection, discipline, patience, all that. . .
And then one day, it suddenly hit me—it really took years in dawning—
A discovery not unlike an astronomer's finding of a bright, new star:

A mother's primary function is to help her children discover
how wonderful they are!

1969—HAPPY EIGHTEENTH

E lizabeth loved her Robert.

I solde was for her Tristan mad.

G alatea lived for her Pygmalion;

H eloise her Abelardo had.

T hisbe had her Pyramus and Romeo, Juliet.

E ve had Adam. Antony was Cleopatra's pet.

E nchanted lovers as each pair might be,

N o pair comes up, my dear, to you and me!

1970—THAT'S WHY I REMIND THEM

A woman cannot be a priest, they say,
because the Lord ordained only men.
If you push it all the way back, what sets a priest apart from all the rest
Is that only he, by uttering the words of Consecration, can incarnate God.

They forget, dear Mother, Mary, that the first who incarnated God
by uttering words, but few
was YOU!

1971—LOVESONG TO GOD

My heart is as full and as swollen as a rain-drenched river—
Full of a million thoughts that crowd within—
Full of discoveries bright with wonder till songs come
Cascading wildly over the brim!

My heart is so full it's spilling over
With singing exultation and light.
It's almost as if God broke open the heavens
To deluge the world with His life!

Oh God, what else can I do but to sing You my love songs
And fling open my all to You? Fill my heart, my life, all of me
O Father, with You!
O Jesus, with You!
O Spirit, with You!

1972—BALANCE

From deep within my heart and welling of my love
I pluck soft, silken words and spin them into gossamer songs—
Loving verses as of silver filigree to give him whom I love.

Alas. His heart can find no earthly use
for such pale, wispy, fragile gifts as these—
And so . . .

From deep within my heart, and welling of my love,
I conjure up fresh, clean, white shirts, a fragrant apple pie,
a brand-new child,
For these are joys that feed the soul of him I love.

And thus while heart spins fancies of dreaming in the silence,
Hands and mind concern themselves with gifts that seek to please.
Joy is wafted all around: the songs give pleasure to the singer
As the Beloved savors love from stronger gifts!

PART II—LIFE FLOWS

As the years ran by, the busy brook of our lives became a river of involvement. Jack was ordained a deacon, our children graduated into college, found their loves, married them, and became parents—making us grandparents, eventually, to 46 wonderful people, big and small (and as of this writing, great grandparents to 38 more). I joined the workforce when I entered the world of the Academy of the Holy Cross, where I have been teaching and working with students since 1979. Jack was active in scouting, both of us and our children in the parish, archdiocese, and Teams of Our Lady. Our lives were aswirl with people!

As a family, we are people people—the introverts and the extroverts both. Surgery for brain cancer slowed Jack down some but he was symptom-free for seven years. We took the big ones and small ones on fun adventures to make memories with them: fishing, museums and art galleries, Chinatown, camping, zoos, hikes, and much more.

1973—HAPPY TWENTY-SECOND

T wenty-two years

W e have lived

E dge to edge, heart to heart.

N o gap has ever been wide enough

T o keep us both apart.

Y ou walk into the room and

S uddenly, all my world lights up with you!

E ven I am so astonished at the

C atch within my heart that

O nly you evoke!

N o barrier could withstand our love's insistence,

D ear, between us there is absolutely no distance.

1974—DELIBERATION

They say this is the time of our lives
When we are most vulnerable to affairs.
I know.
After twenty-three years of togetherness,
I feel a need
For heart-skipping, breath-stopping excitement
Such as we felt in our younger years.
I am resolved to sense that thrill again,
Have that affair.
Feel new!
And then it dawns on me—
The only man who can give me these,
The only man I want to share
Such a lark with, dear, is
YOU!

1975—INVITATION

I would live life
stripped to its barest elements,
Its fundamentals,
Its essence.
To savor every breathing moment,
Not to let it pass:
The depths, the heights,
The tumult, the peace,
Possession, loss,
The ecstasy, the tears,
Dreaming, awaking,
Exulting, aching,
Missing nothing,
Drinking every drop of living to be had.
My, heart, my mind, my arms are open, Life,
I am capacity—

        Be Flood!

1976—WHAT DO THEY CALL THIS AIR MANEUVER?

Sometimes, Lord,

Nothing at all makes sense.

There seems to be no wherefore or whyfor

To anything in life.

I simply want to pull up the covers

And die.

My heart is so weary,

My soul so bleak,

My life so starkly nothing.

Love is only a word

And people merely sources of heartache and pain.

I think of how Eskimos die,

And how pleasant it would be

To simply walk out into the snow

And let go ...

But something within

Prompts me to reach my hand out in the darkness

And then You, Lord, seize me

And my numb, dumb, dispirited soul

Comes leaping into life

And soaring out of the muck and mire

Through and above the clouds

Breaks into the light

The radiant, sunlit blue

And I sing and I sing and I sing—

      Life, I am bigger than you!

1977—LINES ON SURFING

Life in the Lord
is surfing free
without fear of falling
and when you fall
to discover
God is the Sea!

1978—LOGIC

I know I do not fully understand you.

And that I anger and annoy, harass and irritate,

Vex and exasperate you.

It might seem strange

But this precisely

Assures me, dear,

That you must love me

Very much.

Because then love alone must keep you here.

1979—PREFERENCE

People heal one another
In different ways.
Some are surgeons—
Seeing the malignancy, instantly
They excise it with directness,
Dispassionately, objectively,
Never letting pity stay the sureness of their hands.

Some heal with herbs
Of wisdom, kindness, patience,
Compassion, understanding—
Slowly, willing to trust
Nature and time to bring
Wholeness and health about.

And then there are those
Who merrily trip through life
Seeing princes and princesses
Hidden and caught fast,
Captive within
Poor ungainly frogs

And kiss them free to be
The nobility that they are.
If I could choose which of these three
I would be, let me be the last.
Not for me the scalpel nor the therapy
The skill, the herbs, the knowledge, the drugs.

I would just like to go through life
Kissing frogs!

1980—HE SET THE PRECEDENT

Jesus was the original frog-kisser.
In fact, He specialized in frogs.
He said that's who He came for:
The halt, blind, sick, sinner,
Publican, whore.

I don't remember His turning any into princes
Though a rich, young man turned sadly away.
He made whole men out of the lame—
So many of Jesus' froggies
Saints became!

Peter, Magdalene, Matthew, Paul,
Down the centuries they come:
Augustine, Camillus,
Olga of Russia, Mary of Egypt,
Raymond of Lull.

Lord, as You come through,
Don't You miss me—
I desperately need You
To kiss
Me.

1981—YOUR GIFT

You dreamt of a woman wearing an apron baking bread, making pies, gingerbread cookies, rich, hearty stews. A woman who gardened, sewed and knitted, crocheted and embroidered, made jellies and jams, canned vegetables and raised chickens.

So I put on my apron, baked bread every day, outdid myself making pies, and cooked to your heart's and tummy's content. I watered and weeded the gardens you planted, sewed clothes for our kids, knitted socks, embroidered and mended, made goodies galore, fed chickens and puppies, for I wanted to be that woman you dreamt of.

I fancied myself a bluestocking. Inept and clumsy with my hands, I favored my mind and dreamt of becoming a writer of poetry and prose. I wrote snippets of thoughts and phrases, stuffing pages of them in a drawer for some later day. For years we did this—juggling dreams that didn't fit together no matter how we tried.

Until, at last, I decided to give up on mine and determined I would be the most domestic woman I knew how to be, writing books be damned. That was the year you prodded and nagged me into a Master's degree, catapulting me into a rich new world of writing and teaching, making true the dream I thought I was laying aside!

1982—INVENTORY

Each night before sleep comes
I take my jewels out from my heart's keeping
and hold them up to the light of my bright joy.
Miser-like, I fondle every treasure as I turn them here and there:
 Two soft brown eyes with laughter gleaming in their depths,
 A radiant smile that quickens my heart so,
 Two sturdy hands so gentle as they touch,
 A warm embrace of which I cannot get enough,
 An elfin sense of mischief that is my sweet distraction,
 A chiseled beauty, God-made, man-strong and tall,
 A heart filled with love for children and youngness,
 A spirit-well of wisdom and faith,
 A gentleness born of quiet courage,
 Stalwart and unbroken still.
 Eleven shining souls born of a love that is good and true,
 Thirty-two rich years shared with this, my most beloved. . .
And as the mists of sleep so softly overcome
It seems to me that heaven will seem familiar
When God has shown me these!

1983—VALENTINE

I love you
for your goodness the depth of which
I feel I have not begun to fathom yet.

I love you
because with you life is good and beautiful and bright.
It makes sense when you are there.

I love you
for all the little ones you planted beneath my heart—
living proofs of the love affair between God and you and me.

I love you
because you stand so tall I can look up to you
close enough that our shoulders touch
yet managing still to place your head upon my heart.

I simply love you.

1984—THIS IS WHY

Sometimes, knowing what I do, I wonder why people ever get married.

There is so much hurt felt and pain given when two people live so closely.

Often, what makes it easier to maintain one's love for someone is precisely distance.

Near enough to touch hands but not so near as to feel the abrasions of each other's edges.

Far enough that our images of each other blur with illusions like an impressionist's canvas.

Then I remember what it is like to lie in the crook of your arm, fuzzy with sleep in the morning

and you awaken me gently to talk and exchange souls a little before taking life on for that day.

Or snuggling up and fitting my body to your back so that you fill my embrace with such fullness

I float on the unbelievable indescribability that is love. And remembering, I purr with gratitude.

The grace is in remembering all that was beautiful and happy and funny and good!

Oh, I know we miss each other's hand when we reach out for each other, as often as we do not.

And there are days we wonder why we bother to keep it up. But, oh, the times, the times

when we reach out and our hands clasp, our hearts touch, and our spirits fully behold the other!

Then I know, yes, I know, why I followed you across the world, sometimes walk through hell with you

And love you still—you fill me with heaven-joy, my Darling!

Oh, how you fill!

1985—MY TALENT

When God was giving out talents, gifts and graces, blessings—
call them what you will,
they came in countless shapes and colors, sizes, forms,
each one lovelier still
than that which came before.
What wondrous things indeed He had in store
for those He loved—us, His beloved children.

He gave out Beauty, Wonder, Courage and Grace,
Serenity, Brilliance, Creativity, Love and Joy—
brightening the world with every rainbow hue! And then at last,
it was my turn, and lo!
He loved me greatly—this, I knew—
because the Gift His Hand held out to me was you, my Darling—
YOU!

1986—OH, WOW!

My heart is simply awhirl with the joy of simply being.
It sings and sings and will not cease its singing.
I am so filled with Your life, O God, I am ablaze
And my soul, winging, traverses time and space!

O Lord, what must heaven be?
Trinity, envelop me!

1987—THE SHADOWS FALL

I was not counting on mortality showing up so soon.
We are still young.

Before you came, I was just zero.
So when you go, will I be zero again?
And you, in typical brevity, simply said:
"Oh, Honey, I cannot be erased."
Praise God! I will be ever graced.

1988—REFLECTIONS ON COMMITMENT

We made our commitment to each other before God.
In my desire to be faithful to you, I keep faith with Him.
Because I want be faithful to Him, I keep faith with you.
You each keep me faithful to the Other.

Without the one I am not sure I'd bother
To keep faith with either one of you; it is so difficult.
But, you incarnate His goodness and He lifts you to His own,
I am not sure I could have better loved either one of you alone.

1989—WHAT IS LOVE?

Love is the going abroad of one's self in one's desire to be one with the
Beloved.
Love is the desiring and endeavoring at all costs to be all one can possibly
be for the Beloved.

Love is delighting in the sight, the nearness of Another who somehow has
the power of lighting up one's heart, one's life, one's world.
Love is accepting the Beloved just as He is.
Blind to nothing but seeing him as God intended him to be,
And with our loving's power, set him free to make intention reality.

Love is one's willingness to do everything possible (and even dare beyond)
to ensure the Beloved's happiness, well-being, and complete fulfillment.

Love is the exchange of looks between Lover and Beloved—
wordless magic between Man—Woman, Parents—Child, Friend—Friend -
Leaving the air between them luminous with joy!

Love has many faces unchanging still: it is always kind—caring,
patient—forgiving, faithful—trusting, generous—giving, joyous—freeing,
listening—seeing, strengthening—healing . . .

Love is God is Love.

1990—PROBLEMS IN MEASUREMENT

I cannot measure out my love for you in stark dimensions you can see
Simply because it reaches out into infinity.
It leaps so high it brushes past the stars
and plunges deep as heart-deep goes.
It stretches farther than the limits of the universe.
"Do or undergo anything," is what I said.

Why pain, suffering, humiliation, indifference,
disdain, rejection, even hate
Would only be as teardrops on a holocaust!

But then it is a foolishness to try and measure loving.
Its reaches cannot be seen nor shown.
It can only be in the core of one's being
Known.

1991—DIAGNOSIS

I've never in my life ever felt so beautiful!
Not even when I was young and comely enough
to catch a young man's eye,
I don't even mean pretty-beautiful at all, or loved-beautiful, not that.
Or even happy-beautiful, for I still fall into my Sloughs of Despond.

There is just this: I feel so filled with Beauty—
the Beauty that penetrates the universe so suffuses all of me,
every particle of my being glows. Fire is singing in my blood!
I believe I'm in love with God!

1992—THANK YOU STILL AGAIN

Love has many faces:

A shared April day shimmering with sunlight . . .
Sitting together before a blazing fire on a wintry night . . .
Walking hand in hand on a summer evening,
moonlight upon us like a benediction . . .
Huddling together in Banneker Woods as the golden leaves
swirl around us in the fall . . .
Our first shared look at our newborn child, our closeness fast as God's . . .
Taking turns rubbing away each other's soreness at the end of day . . .

Then, too, there are the times when
Love must be a surgeon ready to excise a cancer that threatens
the Beloved's wholeness, the integrity of our love.
Darling, though I might wince and whimper when your scalpel falls,
please know
that for your gift of unfailing honesty;
for giving me the security of knowing
You never lie to me however truth may hurt,
I thank you with my trusting, I bless you in my heart!

1993—NEW REASON

There was a time I clung to you from need.

Today, I look to be with you for another reason entirely:

No longer from compulsion born of needing but because I choose to.

I want to be with you

because with no other meanings

but just as you yourself,

       You joy me!

1994—THE SHADOWS RETURN

I thought we had beaten the scourge of cancer—I was wrong.

It is back so we begin again.

In typical fashion you are game for the challenge,

Willing to beat your opponent in any game.

You are allowed no weapons save healthy eating, clean living, pure grit.

You rise to every encounter with your great heart, strong and fit!

1995—I AM A REALIST

I am not deceived.
I am no child.
I have no illusions.
Life is not one endless, radiant joy.
I have walked through too much muck
And fallen on too many rocks
To believe this to be true.

But there is this—
The heart-splitting joy so far outweighs the pain,
The dazzling sunlight after rain
Unfailingly shines through.
I face the darkness with open arms and without fear

For light and darkness both, my God, are You!

PART III: ON TO ETERNITY

When the cancer recurred in 1995, this time in both brain and lungs, surgery, chemo, and radiation were all contra-indicated. Jack launched into the macrobiotic diet with a will and was able to have two and half years of high quality time before he headed Home. The family gave him all the love, time, and attention that he could slurp up. We never saw anyone fill his last days with such determination, packing them with all the life and good memories they could possibly hold.

After our forty-six years together this side of heaven, I have spent the years since trying to forge a life without him. I "retired" in 2000, taught in Papua New Guinea in 2001, then in the Philippines for a semester in 2003. I was asked to return to Holy Cross in 2004 and trotted right back. What I have found is that there is no such thing as living without him. We will have been together seventy years in 2020, and he cannot be extricated from me. Our daughter Bim got it right early on: "Mom, you just have to learn how to be married to each other when he is already in eternity and you are still in time." It is doable.

1996—WHAT IS SPOUSAL LOVE?

It is love that wishes to be total: physical, mental, emotional, spiritual.
  It longs and strives for complete oneness: in body, mind, spirit, heart.
  It looks for the sharing of nights and days, luminous grace;
  Bed and board, joys to hoard;
  Thoughts and feelings, laughter—tears,
  Hopes and fears, dreams and fancies, values, ideals, beliefs and doubts,
  Convictions and concerns, bouts
  Of sadness, shadows dark,
  Exultation, sunlit mornings, song of lark!

  Spousal love is immersing in the other, bringing forth new life,
  Beginning in heart pressed to heart, then turning out
  Into giving, going abroad, spilling over
  Because the loving hollows out the initial tightness of hearts new to love,
  Softening it to almost liquid flow, like blood,
  Shed for love of others, as Someone did, once upon a cross.
  Spousal love separates the dross of selfishness
  From the essence, lifting human desire to a Power
  That transforms fruit from flower, meadow from sod.
  Spousal love is loving the Other with the love of God.

1997—NOT YET

It will come soon enough
I am not going to grieve as yet.
The jury is still out.
There is still so much to be done:
Dance, fish, sing, shout!
There's a lot of light still.
Night will come soon enough.
There's a chill in the air
But the storm is not yet here.
I will milk all the joy
We have left to us yet
And mine every moment,
Squeeze all I can get
From being with you that I can hold on to
When you shall have gone away from me.
I will not cling
I will just sing
The song that is we:
You and me.
I cannot listen to the clamoring of my frantic heart.
Not now . . .
The darkness, the storm and bitter cold.
In the meantime, let us hold each other tight
Against the dimming of the light
While there is time left to us still
We will . . .
I have sweeter things to do
Like touching you, memorize your face

Stamp it indelibly in my heart,

Clasp you to me so tightly and challenge death

to pluck you from my arms if he dare.

Giving you to God without reserve

And with the same breath beg Him for the miracle

Of your return to the fullness of life.

I will not grieve yet . . .

1998—MOONSCAPE

My once-round world
Is now concave,
The hole in it so great
It has become a sea of tears
Fogged over with fears
Drowning me in the darkness
The starkness
Chilling
Killing
The last vestiges of
The life I loved and knew so well—

This must be hell.

1999—LAMENT

I dread night most—
The time I used to love best,
When, after a long, hard day, I would slip in beside you
And curl my body against yours (always extra warm)
Tucking my legs under your own
Snugly custom-fit together.
I would sigh and purr in delicious bliss and say,
"I love being married to you—
This is my most favorite time of day."
And now, my absolute least.
I never miss you so much as then.
All day, I can hold loneliness and grief at bay
Until this hour I so dread:
For then my need for you floods in so I can hardly breathe.
You are not here to hold.
I am so cold.
I know you are near—
You are here—
Your presence evident all day—
But at night, I need to hold you and be held . . .
Lord, how long do we have to be apart?
How do I live without my heart?

2000—HAPPY FORTY-NINTH!

F ifty years ago, we re-met, girl and boy now become woman & man.

O vernight, a flame was lit that goes on burning still

R aining sparks that ignite life wherever they land

T o bring light to shadows, emptinesses fill,

Y oung energy where strength falters, hope where it is gone,

N ew dreams for the desperate to dare and build on—

I   n that flame, God-life began in the love of one woman, one man

N urturing numerous children over the years by God's desire

E ngulfing our corner of the world with Heaven-fire!

2001—MADANG SONG

(written during a year of teaching in Madang, Papua New Guinea)

The churning grief has gone the way of storms.
Old loves, new loves flutter at the periphery of my life—
butterflies to marvel at on a summer morn.
I am coming to terms at last with the truth
that ultimately I am alone, and
do not have to unceasingly ache for Another.
I am not in pain.
I feel as fresh as last night's rain.
My life is awakening—
Pink and gray as this morning's dawn,
Birdsong filling the air,
dew on the new-mown grass
as I wend my way
to Morning Prayer.

2002—I WONDER

I wonder if I will ever feel beautiful again.
It was you who made me beautiful.
Your believing I was worth loving
made me glow.
Just to know that I was in your high esteem
Allowed me to dream
I was of value, that I had worth.
Pleasure and mirth gave me a brightness
that would not have been there
had you not loved me.
And now that you are no longer here
in the world of men, I fear I will never ever
feel beautiful again.

2003—INDIVISIBLE

You would have to snip, one by one, 94 threads

to sever the bond we have woven over 47 years

or slip them apart to undo the fabric of our love.

Even then, the spirit of our oneness will blaze high aflame.

You could not put that fire out

any more than you can separate

the smoke from a smoldering brand

from that of the one burning beside it.

There is nothing can dissolve

The magic, the oneness of

Unbelievable Us!

2004—BITTERSWEET

One sweet thing about being bereft
is the discovery of what is left:
The grime of memories dries and flakes off
leaving only the original beauty
of the first flush of love,
untrammeled by shadows of loss and pain.
Just love again—
sweetness and dew, freshness and newness of you.

2005—DECISION

(This was the year I professed as a Secular Franciscan.)

The ways to God are many—
Which should I take for mine?
I ask the saints—their answers vary,
I want to love in a straight line.

The shortest distance twixt two points
Is a line that's straight and true.
God's "idiot," Francis, loved Him thus
Lord, let me love You that way too.

2006—RETREAT REFLECTION

"Think of a time when you experienced a powerful love. It can be a time when you were giving the love or being loved. Looking back on that time, would you say that God was present? Describe your experience."

Being loved by and loving you
Was being immersed in God Himself
For it was you who made me understand
What being loved by God meant.
You were sent to put skin on Him,
Incarnate His reality,
To make me understand that love
Was not some romantic idyll,
Wisp of fancy fashioned by an adolescent mind.
Your love was fierce and kind,
Seeing blind to all my flaws
Loving me on despite them.
Our love generated life
In joy and strife, it burgeoned,
Exploding into mirth and song,
Strong with the steel of knowing
That love is always a choice.
How I rejoice
At remembering how good we were together!
You demanded of me my best.
You were also the rest
My spirit could alight on.
You are not gone.
You cannot be—your love enfolds me still

Even as the air I cannot feel

Nor see—I am enveloped by you

Proof that love is stronger than death—

God's own breath keeping me filled with life.

Bereft as I am,

My love for you is a dam

Of tears breaking I can hardly endure,

But I am sure as the day is true

God becomes reality to me

In my loving and being loved by you.

2007—INESCAPABLE

You have become sunlight—
  bright,
  all-surrounding,
  warming me all over.
You are dust-washing rain—
  refreshing the dryness,
  slaking the thirst,
  the tears releasing the unspeakable pain.
The missing eases now that I see
  you are as air—unseen, yet there,
  sustaining life—the Spirit's breath
  transcending death.
Love, cover me!

2008—TEN YEARS AGO, YOU LEFT

Today, I will not think
  Maybe, tomorrow.
  Maybe postponing sorrow
  Will make it shrink.
  I'm afraid of what will happen
  If I consent
  To one pang of longing,
  The merest tinge of pain,
  One littlest drop of rain . . .
  So, very carefully,
  I shall walk today
  And not allow myself
  Anything stronger than
  A muted,
  Very faintest,
  Dull and listless
  Gray.

2009—RE-DEFINITION

Just as indelibly as our genes
   are fixed in our children,
   you are embedded in me.
   So much of who I am now
   is so entwined with you.
   I cannot tell which is my essence,
   which is who.
   Much of the good I carry,
   you gave.
   Much of the not-so-good in me
   that is no longer there,
   you took away.
   Maybe, since you are
   no longer physically here
   I should redefine myself
   as I am without you.
   Tell me, first,
   how do you separate dew
   from the water it falls into?

2010—LOVE IS

Love is not a pitcher
that becomes empty
when the water it contains
is all consumed.

It is a live spring
that keeps flowing
from some deep source within
that feeds it.

Love is the sea
that centuries of sunlight
cannot evaporate,
it is so vast.

Love cannot be exhausted
or used up
or ever totally consumed
because it has no limit.
Love is infinite.

2011—IMMORTAL BELOVED

You cannot be erased
Any more than air can
Or sky or earth.
You gave birth
To the best of me long ago
And so you live
As long as I do
For the finest part of me
Is you!

2012—LONG DISTANCE LOVE

I had forgotten
Love is stronger than death,
That cessation of breath
Does not mean life's ending.
Sometimes, as I lie in deepest night,
Eyes shut tight
Not wanting to think of you
To avoid the hurting,
You reach for me
From heaven-far,
And somehow,
   There you are!

2013—WILL I EVER GET OVER YOU?

Will the time ever come
When that deep of me
That calls to you
And you respond to
Will fall silent?
Will I no longer look back
Someday to those times
We walked the land together
Hand in hand?
Will I get to singing songs
That do not bring you to mind?
Will the moment come
When I no longer feel you
Surrounding me as air?
Should that day dawn, I know
I do not want to be there.

2014—WHO AM I?

I remember me
  Before you:
  Chaos in person
  Without direction
  Out of focus
  Ill defined
  Amorphous mass
  Uncontrolled
  Edges erose . . .
Then you came, and
  In the messy swirl
  Of vanity, anger, sloth,
You saw
The outlines of a rose.
Out of the confusion,
Definition.
Out of the hat, Magician,
You pulled woman out of brat,
Wife-mother from girl,
From promise, fruition.
God made me,
And gave me to you
So I could come true!

2015—HOW?

You did it
By loving me,
Pure and simple.
No fancy strategies—
Just love, strong and true.
You saw my flaws
And hammered them
Into strengths
Such lengths you went to
To make me stand
Proud, tall, and strong.
You turned my melancholy
Into light and song.
Your love for me was like God's:
Creative:
From nothing, Someone.
Like His, redemptive:
You plucked me from hell,
By loving me well.
Like His, sanctifying
My ordinariness into transformation.
Together, we raised a nation!
From the sod
Of your single-minded loving,
You grew me on to God!

2016—I AM EQUAL STILL

Your presence
in my life made me strong
made me hear the song
life sings
in the heart of things
so that I no longer feared it.
As long as I had you beside me
I knew I would be equal
to whatever lay in store—
and now that you cannot be
beside me anymore,
I discover I am equal still
for I keep your spirit
strong
inside me.

2017—LAST WALTZ

It was almost midnight.
We were waiting to watch the ball drop
in Times Square to mark the end of 1997.
You lay in bed quietly, quite spent
with the struggle to live and barely able to move.
But when the first chords of Guy Lombardo's "Auld Lang Syne"
Sounded, you rose and standing beside the bed
You reached for my hand and said, "Let's dance…"
Put your other hand around my waist and we waltzed
As we did many a time through the years.
We were back in the ballroom where we first held
each other in the sweet embrace that waltzing allowed.
Then, we twirled around with grace and ease.
This time I had to help you twirl and swing you round,
sick as you were, approaching your life's end.
You were still every inch the dashing prince
I had so hopelessly fallen in love with decades before.
Nothing could snuff out your unerring sense of romance
Seven weeks before you went on Home, we danced
Unencumbered by your weakness or pain.
Now I look to the day when we can waltz again
To the lilting strains of "Auld Lang Syne"

      In Paradise this time.

2018—WIFESONG

I love you with the fullest love I am capable of.
I shall try and learn to sense your every need
And meet them the best I can
By listening to your being
With all of mine.
I shall cherish you
With all the tenderness
My heart possesses,
Weep with you when you grieve
And love away each ache,
Uphold you when life is filled with stress.
I shall gentle you with all my strength
And be your strength most gently,
Gift you with my rejoicing
In celebrating you.
And upon this I would hang the stars
That are the years we still have
Left to us which is
Forever.

2019—PRAYER

We began with an astonishing love for each other that startled us both.
We nurtured, protected, and safeguarded it through its growth.
We would not allow life nor anyone to batter it down.
Whatever life threw it, it steadfastly held its own.

We did not allow each other to ruin what together we built.
No matter what life dealt us, we both loved to the hilt.
You invented, kept alive, and bolstered our love, dearest God.
And we drank every drop of loving to be had.

I really think You invented this love;
We would not have been able to do so on our own.
Left to ourselves it would have broken and withered away.
The strength and power could not have grown.

Without Your love to guide us, we would not have forgiven.
Without You beside us, what measly love we would have given!
You wrote our love story in our hearts with Your pen.
Please keep it going through eternity, Lord. Amen.

Made in the USA
Middletown, DE
07 February 2020